MEXBOR
AND SWINTON
TROLLEYBUSES

Colin Barker

Series editor Robert J Harley

MP Middleton Press

Front cover picture: Typifying the post war fleet, Sunbeam 27 waits at the Conisbrough High terminus in Welfare Avenue with the indicator set ready for the return journey to Manvers Main. 27 will turn round immediately to the rear of the photographer's position and take a sharp left hand turn at the end of the avenue that can be seen in the distance. (G Lumb)

Rear cover picture: Sunbeam 38 climbs Castle Street on the final stages of its journey to Conisbrough High with the towering keep of Conisbrough Castle on the skyline above the trees. (G Lumb)

Published September 2008

ISBN 978 1 906008 36 9

© Middleton Press, 2008

Design Deborah Esher

Published by
> *Middleton Press*
> *Easebourne Lane*
> *Midhurst*
> *West Sussex*
> *GU29 9AZ*
Tel: 01730 813169
Fax: 01730 812601
Email: info@middletonpress.co.uk
www.middletonpress.co.uk

Printed & bound by Biddles Ltd, Kings Lynn

Photograph Credits:
Some unconventional attributions have been demanded by a few contributors to this album.

CONTENTS

INTRODUCTION AND ACKNOWLEDGMENTS

Having completed my book on the joint trolleybus systems of Grimsby and Cleethorpes for this Middleton Press series, my thoughts turned to other joint trolleybus operations for my next project. After some deliberation I began to consider the joint operations of Rotherham Corporation and the Mexborough company but decided that both had enough scope for their own individual volumes.

The Mexborough and Swinton system had the attraction of an all single deck fleet that operated in the then heavily industrialised South Yorkshire coalfield which has provided many impressive photographs of the industrial landscape in which their trolleybuses operated.

Single deck trolleybuses were a rarity in the United Kingdom and the only vehicles I came across were the Guy trolleybuses of Hastings Tramways seen in this seaside town during my formative years. This provided a connection with Mexborough and Swinton as the company purchased six of these vehicles from Hastings during the 1939-1945 War, as did my hometown of Derby where I can just remember seeing them in service.

This album is not intended to be a detailed history of the system, but a pictorial journey which should bring back memories to older generations who travelled on the trolleybuses and illustrate to younger people an important period of the area's social history.

Virtually all the photographs used are from the collections of enthusiast photographers or copyright holders, who have been generous in allowing their reproduction and due accreditation has been given with each view. It has been impossible to identify the source of a minority of views but I hope the originators will accept their efforts have been used in good faith to enhance this publication to a wider audience. I have endeavoured to minimise views used in earlier publications.

Having never seen the system in operation, and being unfamiliar with the area, I have been heavily dependant on local enthusiasts and my thanks go to Paul Fox and Charles Hall for providing answers to my interminable questions and points of detail. Paul, Derrick Vernon (General Manager at Mexborough 1954-1966) and Geoff Warnes read through the first draft and made a number of constructive suggestions. The Rotherham, Doncaster and Newham libraries plus Beaulieu Motor Museum also provided information. Thanks also go to John Gillham for allowing me to use his map, Terry Russell for the excellent vehicle drawings, Eric Old for sample tickets and the Omnibus Society's Walsall Library for timetables and fare chart. Last, but not least, thanks go to my wife Maureen, for her support and for polishing my text into a form usable by the publisher.

I have thoroughly enjoyed preparing this volume and my research visits to the area bought into sharp focus my GCE studies of the early 1950s, where one of the Geography subjects was the South Yorkshire coalfield. These visits also highlighted the startling changes in the industrial landscape, particularly mining, which have occurred in the 47 years since the trolleybuses of Mexborough and Swinton ceased to operate.

For a more comprehensive history of the Mexborough and Swinton operation readers are referred to the following: -

British Bus and Tram Systems No 33 by Charles C Hall | *Rotherham and District Transport by Charles C Hall*
in Buses Illustrated Nos 80/81 (1961) 82 (1962) | *Volumes 1, 2 and 3 ISBN 0 90366 89 8, 92 8 and 93 6*

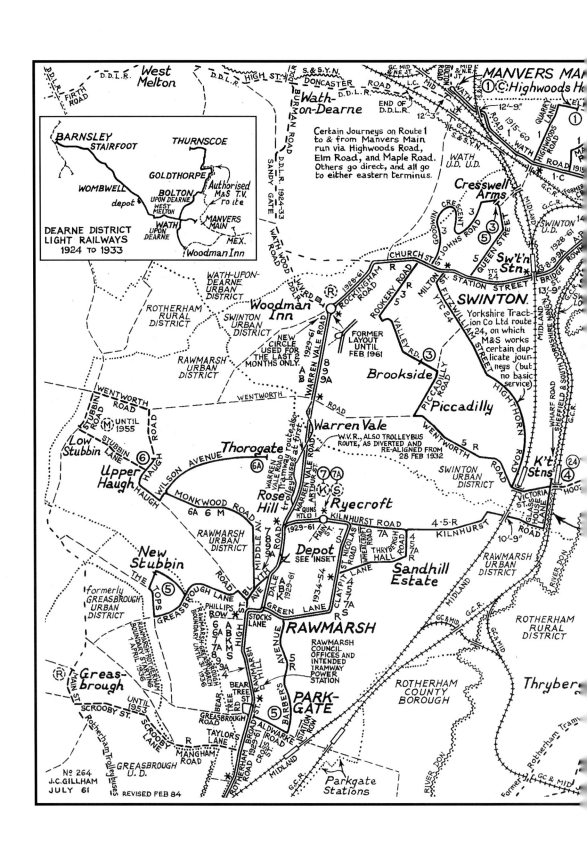

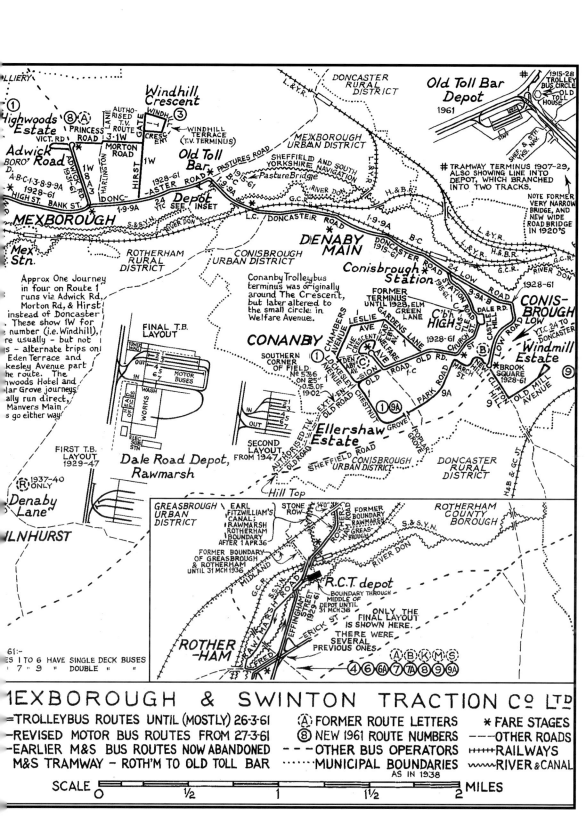

MEXBOROUGH & SWINTON TRACTION Cº LTD

=TROLLEYBUS ROUTES UNTIL (MOSTLY) 26-3-61   Ⓐ FORMER ROUTE LETTERS   ✱ FARE STAGES
=REVISED MOTOR BUS ROUTES FROM 27-3-61   ⑧ NEW 1961 ROUTE NUMBERS   —— OTHER ROADS
=EARLIER M&S BUS ROUTES NOW ABANDONED   — — OTHER BUS OPERATORS   +++++ RAILWAYS
M&S TRAMWAY – ROTH'M TO OLD TOLL BAR   ······ MUNICIPAL BOUNDARIES   ⌇⌇⌇ RIVER & CANAL
                      AS IN 1938

SCALE   0   ½   1   1½   2 MILES

GEOGRAPHICAL AND
HISTORICAL SETTING

The area covered by the Mexborough and Swinton system lies on the higher ground to the west and north of the River Don. It followed a road running north from Rotherham through Park Gate, Rawmarsh, Swinton to Mexborough where it joined a road running east to west between Doncaster and Barnsley; the latter provided access to Manvers Main, Denaby and Conisbrough.

Historically, Roman remains have been found in the Swinton area and a Roman fort existed at Templeborough. The imposing remains of Conisbrough Castle have a heritage that goes back to Norman times with the current keep probably dating from around 1180.

Undoubtedly the key feature to the growth and development of the area was the discovery of coal which was mined as early as the 1600s; early mining methods used bell pits, opencast and drift methods. This eventually led to the development of the South Yorkshire coalfield with its many mines, which in turn spawned other industries that used coal. These included steel, pottery, glass and brick making and hence the transport infrastructure developed to serve these industries.

First was the use of waterways by making the River Don navigable and the construction of associate canals that lead to a local boat building industry. The area was not on the main north/south stage routes and this was repeated with the advent of the railways with the important routes passing to the east and west of the area. The first railway connection was a line from Sheffield to Rotherham opened in October 1838. The rapid growth of railways resulted in a heavy concentration of lines which, whilst providing passenger services, were mainly focused on the movement of coal with the consequent decline of canal transport.

All of the above lead to the rapid urbanisation of the area as people moved to support the growing industries. This in turn was the catalyst for the early tramway proposals culminating in the legal creation of the Mexborough and Swinton Tramway Company in 1902, although it did not become operational until 1907.

HISTORICAL BACKGROUND
TO PUBLIC TRANSPORT

As early as 1876 a horse tramway was proposed from Rotherham to Park Gate situated at the bottom of Rawmarsh Hill. This was withdrawn and resurrected in 1881 under the Rotherham, Park Gate and Rawmarsh Tramway Act whose powers lapsed. With the advent of electric power a number of tramway proposals were made and construction eventually commenced in August 1905 running from the Rotherham railway bridge boundary northwards through to Park Gate and subsequently on to Rawmarsh, Swinton, Mexborough and to the Old Toll Bar at Denaby.

The line was constructed by the National Electric Construction Company Ltd (NECC), opened on 6th February 1907 to Park Gate, and through the other towns to the Old Toll Bar on the 3rd August of the same year. Initially sixteen cars were used and operated by the Mexborough and Swinton Tramways Company. The latter had been incorporated by Act of Parliament in 1902 and promoted by the Mexborough and Rawmarsh Construction Syndicate Ltd, which went bankrupt and was taken over by NECC.

Electrical supply to the trams was via the road mounted Dolter surface contact system rather than using overhead wire as installed in Rotherham; it proved to be unsatisfactory. The company therefore converted to overhead power supply in 1908 and joint running with Rotherham Corporation to Park Gate commenced on the 20th October.

The original 1902 powers allowed for a branch line from Mexborough to the Manvers Main colliery but they were allowed to lapse. A charabanc was hired from an associate company in 1910 to run beyond Manvers Main and between Old Toll Bar and Denaby village but was soon withdrawn after objections from Mexborough Council. The company then began to examine the possibility of railless traction (trolleybuses) and the 1913 Mexborough and Swinton Tramways Railless Traction Act authorised two routes out of the six proposed, namely from the Old Toll Bar, Denaby to Conisbrough and from Mexborough to Manvers Main. The two routes, which were not connected, were opened on 31st August 1915 using three single deck Daimler trolleybuses which were housed in a new small tram/trolleybus depot at the Old Toll Bar terminus. Access from the depot to the Manvers Main route, and probably to the main depot at Rawmarsh, utilised a trailing skate in the tram track. Thus began the first company owned trolleybus system in the country.

The 1914-1918 War led to staffing problems and in April 1916 the routes were closed down, only to be reintroduced shortly afterwards in order to provide transport to the collieries, which were very important to the war effort. To support this activity a second hand Daimler trolleybus was purchased from Stockport Corporation. All this good intent was thwarted by a lack of spares/skilled staff and the system was again closed down until the route to Manvers Main was reopened for short periods in December 1919 and the Spring of 1920; full service resumed in early 1921. Apart from a short period in 1921 the Conisbrough route did not resume until March/April 1922. In this year the company introduced its first motorbus, excluding the earlier hired charabanc experiment, and two AEC trolleybuses plus a further one in 1924, although the latter did not enter service until 1926; these eventually replaced the original vehicles.

The short lived Dearne District Light Railway opened in 1924 and reached Manvers Main some little way from the trolleybus terminus, plus a branch to Woodmans Inn on the Mexborough system. At this time various tramway/light railway schemes were considered including through routes to Sheffield, Barnsley and Doncaster but they came to nothing.

The company decided to convert the tramway system to trolleybuses. A Bill was submitted to Parliament and in December 1925 a Garrett demonstrator was evaluated followed by a

Ransomes in November 1926. Following the incorporation of the Act in 1927 the first six Garretts were delivered early in 1928, followed by a further nine from the same supplier later in the year. A further delivery of twelve Garretts followed in 1929 plus three in 1930.

The first conversion was between Mexborough (Montague Arms) and Denaby in January 1928, thus connecting the original two routes, followed by the section between Mexborough and Woodman Inn in November 1928. This left the section between Rotherham and Woodman Inn operated by trams. The final conversion of this section, which included a short extension along Kilnhurst Road to the Ryecroft area of Rawmarsh, allowed the closure of the tramway system on 10th March 1929. As a result of the 1929 Act the company name was changed to the Mexborough and Swinton Traction Company and the joint operation with Rotherham ran through to Mexborough. In January 1931 the NECC holding company was acquired by the British Electric Traction Company (BET).

New termini were introduced at Conisbrough Low (Brook Square) and Conisbrough High (Conanby) to replace the original terminus and on 28th June 1931 an extension was opened off Bank Street Mexborough along Adwick Road to serve new housing and provide easier turning facilities. Earlier in 1931 a "round the houses" loop was constructed at Park Gate to allow short working from the Rotherham direction. In February 1932 trolleybuses used the newly opened Warren Vale between Rawmarsh and Swinton, which replaced the old narrow hilly road that had been the scene of an earlier serious tram accident. The final extension to the system came on 15th October 1934 when double wiring was introduced from the bottom of Stock Lane Rawmarsh to the Ryecroft terminus via Green Lane, Claypit Lane and St Nicolas Road, thus providing two routes to the Kilnhurst Road terminus. This gave a total service mileage of 24.3 miles (38.9 km).

Further additions to the fleet included six secondhand English Electric vehicles from Nottinghamshire and Derbyshire Traction in 1937 and six Guys from Hastings Tramways in 1942, although not all of the latter ran in service.

The next new delivery was in 1943 comprising six utility Sunbeams finished in grey livery and with spartan internal fittings. After the war these were repainted in a new livery of green and cream replacing the old dark red/brown colour scheme. Further deliveries of Sunbeam trolleybuses occurred in 1947 (18), 1948 (12) and 1950 (3), which allowed the older vehicles to be withdrawn.

During 1948 new wiring was introduced to the narrow roads in the Conisbrough Castle area to allow one-way operation but a proposed extension along Adwick Road to Windhill never progressed. In 1953 the company was incorporated as the Mexborough and Swinton Traction Company Limited making it a limited liability company.

The nationalisation of the electricity supply industry in 1948, the development of post war housing estates, the greater flexibility of motorbuses, and the increasing cost of overhead equipment as the number of UK trolleybus systems declined, all led to the company depositing a Bill in 1959 to discontinue the use of trolleybuses and substituting motorbuses. Thus the company was the last statutory private road passenger transport undertaking in the country to seek and obtain an Act of Parliament in order to change its mode of operation from electric traction to diesel power.

Earlier, in September 1954, the Rotherham - Rawmarsh (Green Lane) service was converted to motorbus operation. Following the Bill being approved by Parliament, the Manvers Main route was converted on 1st January 1961 and the remainder of the trolleybus operation was withdrawn on 26th March 1961. So ended nearly 54 years of electric traction through these South Yorkshire towns, with almost 46 years operated by trolleybuses less some early gaps due to the 1914-1918 War.

Service letters:

A   Rotherham – Mexborough (Adwick Road)
B   Rotherham – Conisbrough Low
C   Conisbrough High – Manvers Main
K   Rotherham – Rawmarsh (Kilnhurst Road)
P   Rotherham – Park Gate
S   Rotherham – Rawmarsh (Green Lane)
    To Rotherham United Millmoor Football Ground.

Abbreviations.

AEC   Associated Equipment Company (trolleybus/motorbus chassis manufacturer)
BET   British Electric Traction Group (transport holding company)
BICC   British Insulated Callender's Cables Ltd (overhead equipment manufacturer)
BTH   British Thomson Houston (trolleybus motor and control equipment manufacturer)
NECC   National Electric Construction Company (tramway construction company)
NTA   National Trolleybus Association
PSV   Public Service Vehicle

Fare chart 1947

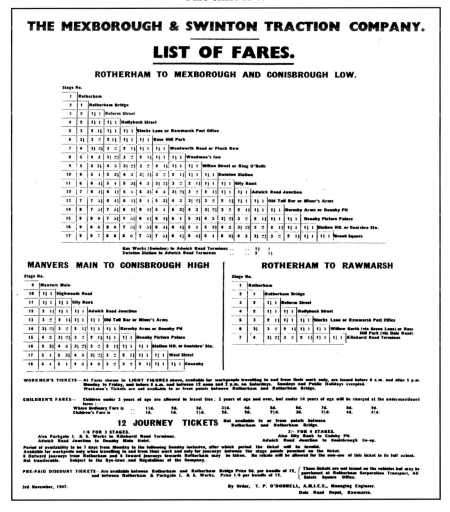

TRAMS TO TROLLEYBUSES

1.   The very early years of the tramway era are illustrated here with Car 13 posing for the photographer at Swinton Common. The studs between the tram tracks indicate the ill-fated short lived Dolter road surface electric current collection system, which left numerous animals electrocuted and trams frequently stranded between contact points. This led to the change to overhead current collection in 1908.
(A D Packer collection)

➜   2. Car 18, delivered with a lowbridge covered top, is seen in Station Street, Swinton on its way to Mexborough with some passengers enjoying the balcony ride. Overhead wiring is now in place and the boom, originally provided for use on the Rotherham overhead wiring, is now used throughout the system. The side-mounted boom was positioned to give headroom under the low bridges that plagued the Mexborough and Swinton system. (S King collection)

➜ 3.   The last Mexborough and Swinton tram, and a replacing trolleybus, pose for the photographer in March 1929 as the section from Rotherham to Woodman Inn was finally converted allowing trolleybuses to run through from Rotherham to Conisbrough. The trolleybus is 44, one of fifteen Garretts delivered in 1928, and the tram is 19 one of the four Brush covered top cars delivered in 1908. (P Fox collection)

ROTHERHAM

4.   We start this photographic journey at the southern end of the system where the beginning and end of the Rotherham town centre loop can be seen in this August 1954 view. The vehicle facing the photographer will move forward and continue along Rawmarsh Road and onward to the town centre terminal point. The vehicle on the right has completed the loop having crossed Grafton Bridge, officially known as Don Bridge, and is about to travel north past the Rotherham Corporation depot in the background to Park Gate and beyond. Rotherham trolleybuses running into service from the depot used the inward wiring over the bridge. (D Smithies)

→   5. Sunbeam 39 is depicted in Rawmarsh Road with the Rotherham depot in the background and the bridge over the River Don on the right.   The overhead junction in the foreground appears to be dual directional as the wiring leaving the top of the picture is the single line into Rotherham; that leading to the left joins the outward wiring towards the depot and Park Gate. Grafton Bridge is still in existence but has been replaced by a later major carriageway across the river. (R Marshall)

→   6.   Two Sunbeams, 38 and 32, inward bound along Rawmarsh Road, pass the brass works of Gummers Limited with a Rotherham Corporation Crossley motorbus following close behind. The first vehicle appears to be minus a front fleet number. (R G H Simpson)

7. The Rotherham Corporation Power Station cooling towers emphasise the industrial nature of the area as Sunbeam 14, closely followed by a second vehicle, passes under single wiring in Rawmarsh Road as it makes its way to the Rotherham terminus in Frederick Street. Note the John Smith's Magnet logo on the erstwhile Thatched House public house. (R F Mack/J Fozard copyright)

8. Sunbeam 27 turns out of Rawmarsh Road into Bridge Street on its way to the Frederick Street terminal stands. On the right is the Bridge Inn, which whilst retaining this name as a secondary identification, is now known as "Nellie Denes". On the left, a Standard 14 car stands in front of buildings that still exist. (R F Mack/J Fozard copyright)

9. Garrett 42 from the 1928 delivery has just rounded the corner at the Bridge Inn and is seen crossing Chantry Bridge over the River Don. This vehicle was out of service for several years following a crash in Rotherham and after rebuilding it acquired the post war green and cream livery; it lasted until 1950. Note that gas is still in use for street lighting. (R F Mack/NTA collection)

10. Garrett 45 or 43 passes the erstwhile Gas Showrooms on the corner of Bridge Street and enters Frederick Street in this March 1943 view, with Rotherham single ended tram 9 immediately in front. Also in view is a Doncaster single deck motorbus. The overhead infrastructure accommodates wiring for both trolleybuses and trams. (Burrows Collection/Newham Museum)

11.   Utility Sunbeam 5 is seen in Frederick Street on Service S to Rawmarsh via Green Lane.   Disused tram track curves round into Howard Street and the nearest set of trolleybus overhead has been removed in this view possibly in anticipation of the change to span wire suspension indicated in the next picture. Both Frederick Street and Howard Street are now pedestrianised. (D F Parker)

→   12.   This June 1955 view illustrates the Rotherham terminus in Frederick Street with Mexborough and Swinton Sunbeam 17 in the foreground destined for Conisbrough Low. Rotherham Daimler 1 (original numbering) is immediately behind and sister vehicle 8 in the far distance. An Austin 12 or 14 travels in the opposite direction under span wires that have replaced the bracket arms seen in the previous picture. The buildings on the right have made way for shops and the Rotherham Interchange. (A D Packer)

→   13.   This view of Sunbeam 39 in Frederick Street is of interest as the destination indicator is set for the short working to Park Gate, Service P. The short working terminus was a "round the houses loop" using very narrow roads (see Pictures 32 and 33).
(D A Jones/London Trolleybus Preservation Society)

↓ 14.   We are now near the end of Frederick Street where the road narrows before reaching Effingham Square. A Rotherham Daimler, rebuilt from a single decker, can be seen turning into the southern section of Effingham Street. Sunbeam 8 waits just beyond the stand for Park Gate (P), Rawmarsh and Kilnhurst Road (K); when these services were operated by Rotherham they were designated Route 8. The conductress on the left appears to be in lightweight summer uniform and in the middle distance the wiring to be able to switch from the centre overhead to that on the left can be seen. Within the female conducting staff some of the employees were as young as sixteen. (W A Camwell)

↑ 15.   In earlier years, other terminal points were used in Rotherham and the next few views cover these locations. This view taken in August 1935 in All Saints Square depicts Garrett 51 destined for Conisbrough Low with Rotherham Corporation 55, a Ransomes Sims and Jefferies, waiting to depart for Kimberworth. Trolleybus drivers did not need a PSV licence, but were required to hold a hackney carriage licence to drive in the Rotherham Corporation area.
(G H F Atkins/ Courtesy & © John Banks collection)

16.   Also seen in All Saints Square is Garrett 43 with passengers boarding via the central entrance. The young boy sits forlornly on what appears to be a flower tub and, to his right, revenue earning advertising can be seen on the entrance step of the vehicle. Shops in the background include John Law & Sons and Horace Brook Fruit and Floral Specialist. Notice that, at the time this pre war photograph was taken, the Rotherham numbers for the joint services were 24 and 25. (G H F Atkins)

17.   At the same location Garrett 37 waits with nearside cab door open and bedecked with ribbons. Two Rotherham Corporation motorbuses are also in view together with a decorated trolleybus from the same fleet. The street decorations were probably to commemorate the coronation of King George VI in 1937, although the decorated trolleybus was fitted out in 1935 and photographs exist with it indicating "Happy New Year". (S L Smith/NTA Brearley collection/P Fox copyright)

18.   This wartime view taken in May 1941 depicts ex Nottinghamshire and Derbyshire English Electric 303, now 67 in the Mexborough fleet, waiting on stand in All Saints Square. A Rotherham motorbus stands in front of Thornton's Chocolate Kabin and war time black and white kerb markings are in evidence, together with what appears to be a turning circle in the overhead wiring. 67 was withdrawn in 1948. (G Baddeley/J H Meredith collection)

19.   For a period between All Saints Square and Frederick Street being used as a terminal point for Mexborough and Swinton trolleybuses, a stand in Bridgegate was used. Sunbeam 27 is depicted waiting at this point prior to departure to Conisbrough Low. (W J Haynes)

20.   Garrett 51 is seen again, this time outside Joseph Peck's department store in Bridgegate, with Sunbeam 21 immediately behind, the former being part of a batch of twelve trolleybuses delivered in March 1929. Note the different styles of livery with 21 in the post war green and cream whilst 51 is still in the original dark red. (F N T LL Jones/P Fox collection)

21.   Returning now to the route out of Rotherham a little further along Frederick Street, Sunbeam 28 moves away from the departure stands before turning left into the northern section of Effingham Street. Note the tarred over tram track and the AEC Regal coach following close behind.
(G Baddeley/
J H Meredith collection)

➜ 22. The iconic clock tower in Effingham Square, known as the "Hastings Clock", having been given by a local businessman of the same name to mark the coronation of George V in 1902, is the centrepiece of this view. Sunbeam 27 moves out of Frederick Street into the northern section of Effingham Street and onwards to Grafton Bridge. The wiring leaving the top of the picture leads to the eastern section of Frederick Street into which the Standard car is progressing. This wiring served the Rotherham routes to Pumping Station, Thrybergh and Silverwood. Power is being fed to the overhead via the section insulators suspended from the bracket arm in the foreground.
(D Jones/London Trolleybus Preservation Society)

➜ 23. At the end of the Rotherham terminal loop, Sunbeam 39 crosses Grafton Bridge over the river in August 1956 as it leaves Effingham Street and is about to make a right turn into Rawmarsh Road and hence pass the Rotherham Corporation depot. The wiring leaving the picture to the right continues along Rawmarsh Road into the centre of Rotherham, as seen in Pictures 5 and 24. The visual indicator to show drivers the setting of the overhead junction for the above can be seen mounted on the traction standard on the left. Tram track is still in place. The Grafton Hotel is depicted in the background and the trolleybus is being followed by Hillman Minx and Ford Popular cars. All the buildings to the rear have been swept away and replaced with a major road scheme. (A D Packer)

24.   This view, also taken in August 1956, is a little further on and looking along Rawmarsh Road with its single set of overhead wiring into Rotherham town centre. Sunbeam 10, in experimental all over green livery, moves across the cobbles on its way to Conisbrough Low. Top left, on the nearside wiring, is the switch that operated the overhead junction further on and was linked to the driver's indicator referred to in the previous picture. New street lighting was being mounted to the traction standards to replace gas lamps when this photograph was taken; an example of the latter can be seen above the base of the right hand boom. The industrial background relating to Rotherham Corporation power station completes the picture. (A D Packer)

→   25. The Rotherham power station buildings again dominate the scene as Sunbeam 34 moves up the incline in Rawmarsh Road to pass over Rotherham Bridge en route to Mexborough on Route A. The Rotherham Corporation depot is on the left, and with the exception of a single car, the road is otherwise deserted. (R F Mack/J Fozard collection)

→   26.   Sunbeam 36 crosses the bridge over the ex Great Central Railway referred to in the previous picture (this was the boundary between the Rotherham and Mexborough systems in the tramway era) before dropping down to pass the Rotherham Corporation depot and thence to the loop into the town centre. The background illustrates the many industrial activities in the Park Gate and Rawmarsh areas. (A D Packer)

PARK GATE

27.   We have now left the Rotherham overhead wiring as Sunbeam 27 leaves the underbridge in Rotherham Road, Park Gate, which carried the ex Midland Railway line to the north. The cat's cradle of wiring over the top of the trolleybus overhead presumably offered protection in the event of a breakage of higher level railway telephone wires. The advertisement on the right suggests that the UK pig industry was facing severe foreign competition even in April 1960 when the photograph was taken. (A D Packer)

➔   28. Sunbeam 33 follows one of the company's Leyland Tiger Cub motorbuses along Rotherham Road towards Rotherham; the latter replaced some of the early trolleybuses. The sale of alcohol is well served with the corner off-licence and two pubs in the background, namely The Forge Inn and The Rail Mill Inn. These names are indicative of the then local industries and the latter is remembered today with a modern roadway named Rail Mill Way. (R F Mack/NTA collection).

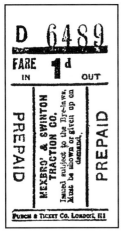

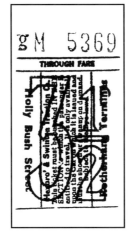

➔   29. At the same location, we see an example of the joint working with Rotherham Corporation depicting Daimler 8; a Hillman Minx car follows close behind. The off-licence on the corner of Reform Street (previously Chapel Street) is advertising four brands of cigarette, two brands of tea plus Magnet Ales and Tizer. (R F Mack/J Fozard copyright)

30. In March 1961, Sunbeam 31 passes the Park Gate steel works on its way to Conisbrough Low against the background of the towering cooling towers. Both the trolleybus, and the Ford 100E Anglia or Prefect car, pass over the works' railway crossing. This entire industrial scene has been swept away and the Gateway Industrial Estate now occupies the site. (A D Packer)

➜ 31. This rear view of Garrett 52 travelling towards Rawmarsh was taken in Broad Street. Tram track is still in place and the corner of Lloyd Street can be seen on the extreme right. Note the imposing gas lamp on the left. (S L Smith/P Fox copyright)

➜ 32. Garrett 50 is seen in Broad Street approaching the overhead junction that led into the "round the houses" short working loop from the Rotherham direction. The wiring led into Greasbrough Road and then along Bear Tree Road and Bear Tree Street before returning into Broad Street. (Commercial postcard/ S Lockwood collection)

33.   Rotherham Daimler 3 is seen on the Park Gate short working loop whilst on a last day enthusiast's tour on 26th March 1961 organised by Geoff Warnes, who read through the original draft of this book. It is leaving Bear Tree Road and turning into Bear Tree Street; the buildings on the left are now demolished and modern family housing occupies the right hand side of the road. (R F Mack/NTA collection)

34.   Sunbeam 37 descends Rawmarsh Hill and moves towards Park Gate on its way to Rotherham in July 1959. The parish church of St Mary the Virgin sits on top of the hill and the corner of Netherfield Lane is bottom right. One of the company's Leyland Tiger Cub motorbuses climbs the hill with an Austin A40 Somerset parked on the left. This section of overhead is one of a number where old 18" (457mm) spacing has been replaced with modern BICC 24" (610mm) twin line hangers. (A D Packer)

35.   Sunbeam 36 has climbed Stocks Lane from the Green Lane/Dale Road junction and rounds the bend into Rawmarsh High Street. The Star Inn forms the backdrop to this view although Stocks Lane is now closed off at this point with through traffic continuing along Blyth Avenue on the left and thence to Dale Road. (R F Mack/J Fozard copyright)

36.   The cobbled incline of Stocks Lane presents no problem for Sunbeam 26 as it moves towards Rawmarsh High Street and onwards towards Park Gate in July 1959. Note there is no support between the twin line hangers mounted from the bracket arm. The Crown Inn is in the far distance at the bottom of the hill at the junction with Dale Road, which was the beginning of the Green Lane loop. Also see Picture 48. (S King)

→ 37.   Sunbeam 32 rounds the bend out of the narrow part of Dale Road into the wider section at the junction with Blyth Avenue in March 1961. The manual folding doors are open and there is a good passenger loading with those at the front sitting on the rearward facing seats behind the bulkhead. In the misty far distance is the main depot and workshop. (L W Rowe)

↓ 38.   Sunbeams 38 and 26 pass each other outside the Rawmarsh depot looking in the Park Gate direction. In the final overhead layout vehicles could exit to travel in either direction but wired access was only from Swinton. (London Trolleybus Preservation Society)

39.   Sunbeam 32 waits in Dale Road with the main depot in the left background. The driver appears to have stopped with a boom under the dead section insulator and may well have to allow the vehicle to roll back down the incline on restarting in order to gain power. Section insulators occurred every half-mile to prevent any power failure in one section affecting adjacent sections of overhead. In the majority of cases this was also the point where electricity was fed to the overhead, which is the case in this view. (A D Packer)

➜   40.   On the brow of the hill at the end of Dale Road and the beginning of Warren Vale, Sunbeam 30 is about to pass under the overhead junction for Kilnhurst Road on the left. To the rear of 30, where the first span wire occurs, the switch can be seen on the right hand wire which allowed drivers to set the overhead junction (known as a frog). A Morris Minor Traveller passes in the opposite direction. (S King)

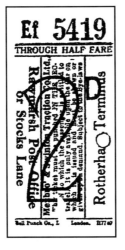

➜   41.   A clear road as far as the eye can see looking towards Woodman Inn as Sunbeams 38 and 27 pass each other in the cutting at the Rawmarsh end of Warren Vale just beyond Kilnhurst Road in March 1961. Between here and Woodman Inn was a fairly rural section of this otherwise urban trolleybus system where speeds in excess of 40mph (64.4 km/h) could be achieved, although with a grave risk of booms becoming de-wired. (S King)

RAWMARSH (RYECROFT/GREEN LANE)

42.   Returning to Picture 40, we are now looking along Kilnhurst Road with Rotherham Daimler 3 approaching the turn into Dale Road on the last day tour on 26th March 1961. The terminus is a little further on and served the Ryecroft area of Rawmarsh, although route indicators displayed Kilnhurst Road Route K. (J C Gillham)

→ 43. The turning circle at the Rawmarsh Ryecroft terminus allowed vehicles to turn in either direction after the Green Lane loop was opened. Sunbeam 13, subsequently used as a training vehicle (see Picture 101), stands in Kilnhurst Road facing towards Dale Road showing Service K in July 1954, whilst a sister vehicle stands beyond the turning circle ready to go round the Green Lane loop on Service S back to Dale Road at the bottom of Stocks Lane. (A D Packer)

→   44.   Another view of the Rawmarsh Ryecroft turning circle with Sunbeam 18 showing Service S turning back towards the wiring for the Green Lane loop and with Main Street on the right. The turning circle overhead incorporates modern BICC 24" (610mm) fittings whilst further along Kilnhurst Road earlier 18" (457mm) spaced wiring is still in place. (A D Packer)

Timetable for November 1948

Service K	ROTHERHAM - RAWMARSH (via Dale Road)											
MONDAY TO SATURDAY :	From ROTHERHAM	5.28	6.10	6.25	6.32	6.50	7.5	7.17	7.47	7.57	8.5	8.25	9.8 a.m. then 10.53 p.m.
	From MAIN STREET	5.20	5.50	6.12	6.30	7.15	7.48	8.7 a.m.

SATURDAY ONLY :   From ROTHERHAM   From MAIN STREET
1.33 p.m. and every 10 minutes until 5.33 p.m.   1.13 p.m. and every 10 minutes until 5.13 p.m.
6.13 „ „ „ „ 20 „ „ 10.53 „   6.33 „ „ „ 20 „ „ 10.13 „ then 10.53 p.m.

SUNDAY :   From ROTHERHAM 5.25 6.43 7.23 a.m. then 10.51 p.m.
            From MAIN STREET 6.23 6.40 7.43 a.m.

45.   An unidentified Sunbeam has left the Kilnhurst Road terminus in the distance and is about to turn left into St. Nicolas Road, and onwards into Claypit Lane, to begin the second leg of the loop back to Dale Road. (D Smithies)

46.   At the end of the second leg of the loop Sunbeam 10 begins the turn out of Claypit Lane into Green Lane in 1954, having climbed from St. Nicolas Road in the background.   (D Smithies)

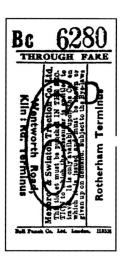

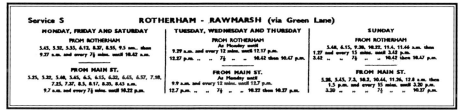

Timetable for November 1948.

47.   Sunbeam 14 has passed under the junction at the bottom of Stocks Lane and is beginning its journey along Green Lane towards Claypit Lane on the circuit to the Kilnhurst Road terminus. The rear destination indicator displays Service S, this being the sole preserve of the Mexborough vehicles. (D Smithes)

48.   We have returned to the bottom of Stocks Lane as Sumbeam 11 approaches the overhead junction for the Green Lane loop where wiring can be seen adjacent to the Crown Inn. The contact to operate the junction can be seen on the left hand negative wire just beyond the bracket arm in the foreground carrying the overhead. Demolition and road alterations at the bottom of Stocks Lane have resulted in a later replacement Crown Inn being built beyond the one depicted. (D Smithies)

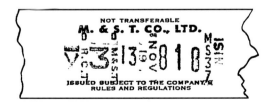

WOODMAN INN/SWINTON

49.   Sunbeam 32 speeds along the wide three lane Warren Vale between Swinton and Rawmarsh inward bound to Rotherham on Service A with the Woodman Inn in the far distance. In February 1932, this stretch replaced a narrow hilly road that was the scene of an earlier serious tram accident; it was the original route taken by the trolleybuses. A Morris Minor saloon overtakes a tower wagon to complete this rural scene taken in April 1960. (R F Mack/J Fozard copyright)

50.   This poor view has been included as it shows the meeting of two systems at Woodman Inn. In the foreground is a tram of the short lived Dearne District Light Railway which terminated at the end of the road before returning towards Wath; beyond is an unidentified Garrett trolleybus of Mexborough and Swinton. When the latter operated trams, there was a physical connection between the two systems with hopes of through running to Rotherham and beyond, but the Dearne trams were too long to negotiate a road dip in the old Warren Vale on the Mexborough system. (M J O'Connor/National Tramway Museum)

51.   With the Swinton boundary in the background, Sunbeam 10 leaves Rockingham Road and approaches the traffic roundabout at Woodman Inn. The roundabout opened in February 1961 and was only used by the trolleybuses for the two months before closure of the system. Note the pre-fab bungalows on the right, now replaced with modern housing, and the rear of a Mexborough & Swinton Leyland Tiger Cub saloon. (A D Packer)

52.   Sunbeam 31 is seen in Rockingham Road moving towards Woodman Inn en route to Rotherham amongst the bungalows and houses of suburbia. The 18" (457mm) overhead spacing had not been replaced with more modern wider fittings in this March 1961 view. (A D Packer)

53.   Sunbeam 31 is seen again leaving Church Street and rounding the bend into Rockingham Road against the background of substantial semi-detached housing in Racecourse Road. The Kings Head public house is to the right of the photographer's position. (S Lockwood collection)

54.   Sunbeam 30 leaves the Rotherham side of the low railway bridge adjacent to the ex-Midland Swinton Station and enters Station Street with the destination showing Rotherham but indicating Service C. British Railway timetables/advertising boards are mounted on the embankment wall with a chalk written display board on the pavement below. The view dates from April 1960. (A D Packer)

55.   A further view of Swinton railway bridge, which carries the line from Rotherham north towards York, has Sunbeam 27 emerging on the opposite side with booms depressed as it climbs up the incline to the canal bridge and Bridge Street. The local Women's Volunteer Service (WVS) clothing store can be seen on the right in this July 1959 view but it has since been demolished. (A D Packer)

56.   The humpback Swinton canal bridge is the setting for this view as Sunbeam 27 is seen again about to head down the incline to pass under the adjacent railway bridge whilst on Service A to Rotherham in April 1960. Note how the 18"(457mm) wiring is carried over the hump using a full width bracket arm and free standing spacers in the top left of the picture. The bridge crosses the Dearne and Dove Canal, part of the Sheffield and South Yorkshire Navigation, and to the right are the Swinton Locks leading into the Mexborough New Cut of the navigation network. (A D Packer)

57.   At the same location, we see a further illustration of the joint working with neighbouring Rotherham as their Daimler 5 clears the top of the humpback bridge inward bound to its hometown. The passing motorcyclist gives a wave to the family on the left. The Waddingtons name in the advertisement has its origins in the business started by the late Victor Waddington, who championed canal transportation in the area and who had a boatyard in Swinton. (R F Mack/J Fozard copyright)

58.   Sunbeam 38 moves along Rowmes Lane towards the canal bridge. The Victorian schools on the left now house a number of retail business units and Talbot Road, on the right, has been widened by the demolition of a number of properties in the view. The motorcyclist positions himself ready to overtake before the days of mandatory head protection. (A D Packer)

MEXBOROUGH

59.   We are now approaching Mexborough and Sunbeam 28 is seen leaving the two ex Great
Central Railway bridges at the end of Rowmes Lane. Beyond the bridges, which had headroom
of 14' 3" (4.34m), is Swinton Road leading into the centre of Mexborough. Currently to the left
foreground of the bridge is the large Stalrad/Ideal Heating distribution centre. (J C Gillham)

60.   Sunbeam 32 has passed under the two railway bridges into Swinton Road and is about to pass under the overhead junction of the Manvers Main route that leaves the picture to the left. 32 will enter the High Street on the right as it makes its way to Adwick Road on Service A. The Midland Bank building on the right has had an extreme change of use as it now houses Coral the bookmaker.
(R F Mack/J Fozard copyright)

➔ 61.   Here we see another example of the joint working with Rotherham as their Daimler 8 turns out of High Street towards Swinton Road in April 1960 on the return journey from Adwick Road or Conisbrough Low (probably the latter).   Note that Rotherham used No. 9 for these services. The lack of clarity is due to the fact that in later years No.8 was displayed for Adwick Road, which was the number allocated for Park Gate and Rawmarsh in earlier years. A Morris "J" Type van is parked adjacent to Timothy Whites, a retailer older readers will remember. (C Routh)

62.   Sunbeam 20 leaves High Street in April 1960 and is about to enter Main Street on its way to Manvers Main on Service C from Conisbrough High. Note that C is shown twice on the destination blinds and that the colliery is the main destination with the town of Wath in brackets. The wiring leaving top right of the picture leads towards Swinton Road and onwards to Rawmarsh and Rotherham. The driver's visual indicator for the setting of the overhead automatic junction is positioned above the traffic lights. One of the two retail chains illustrated still trades today. (C Routh/R F Mack/J Fozard copyright)

63.   With the exception of Sunbeam 25, the Mexborough High Street is deserted in this view suggesting that the photograph was probably taken on a Sunday. 25 is moving towards Swinton Road and the contact to operate the overhead junction can be seen just in front of the twin line hanger at the top of the picture. High Street is now pedestrianised and a parallel dual carriageway runs to the right of the buildings in this view. (C Carter)

64.   Sunbeam 21 destined for Rotherham, and with a sister vehicle behind, waits at the twin stops in Bank Street. In earlier years, the Prince of Wales Theatre was to the right of this view. (C Carter/NTA Brearley collection)

MANVERS MAIN

65.   Returning now to the High Street/ Main Street junction in Mexborough, this September 1929 view depicts Garrett 36 passing under first generation overhead as it enters Main Street on the way to Manvers Main. Note the destination blind indicates Wath in brackets, although the terminus was some way short of this village. Tram track can still be seen in the granite setts and a Morris Oxford car passes the policeman on point duty. The Garrett lasted until 1947.
(S L Smith/NTA Brearley collection/P Fox copyright)

Timetable for November 1948. Note the early start for miners and steelworkers.

Service C — MANVERS MAIN - CONANBY

	MONDAY											TUES., WED. AND THURS.					
MANVERS		4.30 every	6.30 every	11.50 every	10.30	10.40	10.50	11.0	11.10			MANVERS	As	6.30 every	1.30 every	10.30 Then	
MONTAGU		4.40 10	6.40 20	12.0 10	10.40	10.50	11.0	11.20	11.20			MONTAGU	Mon.	6.40 20	1.20 10	10.40 at	
OLD TOLL BAR		4.35 mins.	6.45 mins.	12.5 mins.	10.45	10.55	11.5	11.15	11.25			OLD TOLL BAR	until	6.45 mins.	1.25 mins.	10.45 Mon.	
CONANBY		4.50 until	5.0 until	7.0 until	12.30	11.0						CONANBY		7.0 until	1.40 until	11.0	
CONANBY		4.15 every	6.20 every	12.25 every	10.35	10.45	10.55	11.5				CONANBY	As	6.20 every	12.25 every	10.35 Then	
OLD TOLL BAR		4.25 10	6.35 20	12.42 10	10.52	11.0	11.30	11.20				OLD TOLL BAR	Mon.	6.35 20	12.42 10	10.52 at	
MONTAGU		4.30 mins.	6.40 mins.	12.47 mins.	10.57							MONTAGU	until	6.40 mins.	12.47 mins.	10.57 Mon.	
MANVERS		4.40 until	5.0 until	5.20 until	6.50 until	12.55 until	11.5					MANVERS		6.50 until	12.55 until	11.5	

	FRIDAY							SATURDAY					
MANVERS	As	6.30 every	11.10 every	10.30 then		MANVERS	As	6.30 every	9.10 every	10.30 Then	
MONTAGU	Mon.	6.40 20	11.20 10	10.40 at		MONTAGU	Mon.	6.40 20	9.20 10	10.40 at	
OLD TOLL BAR	until	6.45 mins.	11.25 mins.	10.45 Mon.		OLD TOLL BAR	until	6.45 mins.	9.25 mins.	10.45 Mon.	
CONANBY		7.0 until	11.40 until	11.0		CONANBY		7.0 until	9.40 until	11.0	
CONANBY	As	6.20 every	11.45 every	10.35 then		CONANBY	As	6.20 every	9.45 every	10.35 Then	
OLD TOLL BAR	Mon.	6.35 20	12.2 10	10.52 at		OLD TOLL BAR	Mon.	6.35 20	10.2 10	10.52 at	
MONTAGU	until	6.40 mins.	12.7 mins.	10.57 Mon.		MONTAGU	until	6.40 mins.	10.7 mins.	10.57 Mon.	
MANVERS		6.50 until	12.15 until	11.5		MANVERS		6.50 until	10.15 until	11.5	

	SUNDAY																
MANVERS		5.40 6.10 7.0 7.30 every	11.0 11.40 12.26 every	10.26 10.38 10.52 11.5			CONANBY	5.10 6.30 7.0 8.0 every	11.30 12.29 every	10.31 10.45 10.59	
MONTAGU		5.50 6.20 7.10 7.40 20	11.10 11.50 12.46 14	10.36 10.50 11.2 11.15			OLD TOLL BAR	5.25 5.37 6.43 7.15 7.45 30	11.45 12.44 14	10.46 11.0 11.15	
OLD TOLL BAR	4.55 5.55 6.25 7.15 7.45 mins.	11.15 11.55 12.53 mins.	10.41 10.55 11.9 11.30			MONTAGU	5.30 5.32 6.50 7.20 7.50 8.30 mins.	11.50 12.49 mins.	10.51	
CONANBY	5.10 6.10 7.0 7.30 8.0 until	11.30 12.10 1.31 until	10.59			MANVERS	5.40 5.42 7.0 7.30 8.0 8.30 until	12.0 1.4 until	11.5	
	B. Sq.										

66.   Former demonstrator AEC 25 is seen parked outside the premises of Groom Brothers in this animated scene in Main Street with the top of the booms extremely widely spaced. Groom Brothers were cycle manufacturers according to a trade directory of the period. Parked in front of 25 there appears to be a steam lorry. The small boy posing for the photographer, the telegram boy on the bicycle, and the smartly dressed gentleman striding out on the right complete the picture. (R Marshall collection)

67.   The lowest under bridge on the system at 12' 9" (3.88m) was immediately before the Manvers Main terminus and Sunbeam 33 is seen here in July 1957 travelling along Wath Road with booms depressed as it passes underneath the structure. The railway line above was originally the Midland and North Eastern Railway Companies' jointly owned Swinton and Knottingley Loop. (J C Gillham)

68.   The importance of the system to the mining industry is illustrated in this view of one of the early AEC's with a full load of end of shift colliers. The Manvers Main colliery complex can be seen beyond the railway embankment that carried the Midland Railway line towards the Barnsley area. The wiring for the turning circle is well illustrated. (NTA collection)

ADWICK ROAD

← 69.   The industrial infrastructure of the Manvers Main colliery area forms the backdrop for this May 1960 view at the terminus of Service C, with Sunbeam 39 on layover before returning to Conisbrough High. This area is unrecognisable today with no evidence of the industrial history depicted in these two views, having been replaced by modern business parks and corporate offices. The low bridge depicted in Picture 67 is the only point of reference today.
(R F Mack/NTA collection)

70.   We now return to the main route at the junction of Bank Street (to the rear of the photographer), with Doncaster Road on the right and Adwick Road on the left.   In the foreground Sunbeam 35 has arrived from the Denaby direction in April 1960 on its way to Manvers Main, whilst an unidentified sister vehicle leaves the Adwick Road branch. To complete the picture a Singer Gazelle overtakes the lone cyclist. (A D Packer)

71.　　This view looks along the length of Adwick Road towards the road junction seen in the previous picture, which is at the bottom of the hill in the far distance. A Rotherham trolleybus descends the hill under bracket arm suspended overhead wiring. (J C Gillham)

72.   This late afternoon view is at the Adwick Road terminus with Sunbeam 26 waiting in the turning circle at the junction with Princess Road. There were plans to extend the overhead further along Adwick Road to the Windhill Estate but this never came to fruition. Note the police box in front of Newton's corner shop, the latter now an off-licence, and the clock tower on the right hand sub-station building. Two Austin A40 vehicles approach with the Countryman version in the foreground. The crew, including the conductress having a crafty cigarette, look towards the photographer; does anyone from the area recognise them? (R F Mack/J Fozard copyright)

Timetable for November 1948.

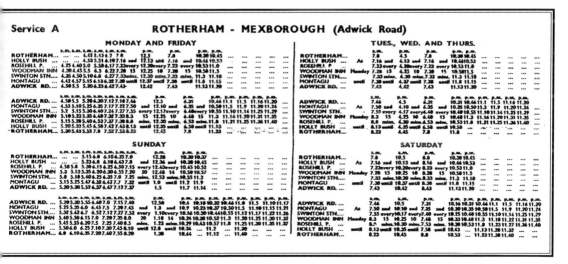

OLD TOLL BAR/DENABY

73.   When the separate early trolleybus routes at Mexborough and Conisbrough were connected as part of the conversion of the whole system from trams to trolleybuses in 1928, a double deck Garrett was loaned from Doncaster perhaps to provide publicity for the manufacturer. Exactly why a double decker was used when there was the low bridge at Manvers Main is not clear. Here, Mexborough & Swinton Garrett 37 from this manufacturer's first delivery passes Doncaster 1 parked with booms down outside the Old Toll Bar depot. (R Marshall collection)

➔   74.   With the entrance to the small Old Toll Bar depot on the left, Sunbeam 37 rounds the bend in Doncaster Road in March 1961 and will shortly pass over the Sheffield and South Yorkshire Navigation bridge, which was of a weight restricted wooden construction when the route was first opened. The area to the rear of 37 was the original trolleybus terminus for the Conisbrough route and the extent of the tramway system from the Mexborough direction. In this area the overhead has been refurbished with 24" (610mm) BICC modern fittings. (A D Packer)

➔   75.   Sunbeam 24 en route to Manvers Main crosses the bridge over the Navigation, referred to in the previous picture, with the Mexborough power station dominating the skyline. The power station no longer exists with the site now being covered by a new road bridge that climbs over the Navigation, River Don and the railway line thus avoiding Denaby level crossing. The wiring leading off to the right leads into the Old Toll Bar depot. (C Carter)

76. With the Denaby rail crossing closed, Sunbeam 27
waits in the queue for the train to pass and the gates to
open so it can proceed towards Old Toll Bar and onwards
to Conisbrough. The frequent crossing closures at this
location caused major disruption to schedules. The signal
box controlling the crossing can be seen on the left and the
footbridge on the right was frequently used by enthusiast
photographers, as illustrated in the next picture.
(J C Gillham)

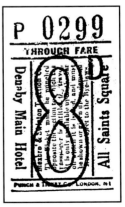

P 0299
THROUGH FARE
Denaby Main Hotel
All Saints Square
8D
PUNCH & TRELT Co. LONDON, N1

77.   Two of the post-war Sunbeams are about to pass each other in Doncaster Road with a Leyland Tiger Cub motorbus on the left.   The roof mounted frame for the booms is well illustrated together with the walkway to the boom retainers at the rear.   The generating buildings and the base of the cooling towers of Mexborough power station complete this industrial scene.   (J Law)

78.   The railway crossing gate at Denaby is closed to road traffic to allow WD locomotive 90456 to move the freight train west towards Mexborough, with the buildings of Denaby Main Colliery on the left. Sunbeam 37 waits for the train to pass with Rotherham Daimler 3 behind on the last day tour. Note the 18"(457mm) spaced overhead, semaphore railway signals and the multi insulated telegraph poles. Automatic barriers now control this crossing as the main road passes to the right over the new bridge. Today, when having passed over the tracks, the road leads to the Dearne Valley Leisure Centre built on the site of the Denaby Main Colliery. (R F Mack/NTA collection)

79. This view shows an AEC, one of the second generation of trolleybuses to be acquired, approaching the Denaby level crossing; they eventually replaced the original Daimlers. In the background, the pit headgear for the colliery can be seen with hoardings advertising places of local entertainment. Pneumatic tyres were fitted to these vehicles in 1927. (R Marshall collection)

CONISBROUGH LOW

80.   This March 1961 view shows where the two Conisbrough routes parted. On the left is Low Road leading to the Conisbrough Low terminus in Brook Square, whilst Station Road on the right leads up the hill to the narrow roads around the castle and onwards to the Conisbrough High terminus in Welfare Avenue. Sunbeam 26 approaches the junction on its way to Rotherham; drivers travelling in the opposite direction could tell the setting of the overhead junction they were approaching by reference to the indicator mounted on the left hand traction standard in the foreground. The rake angle of the traction standard immediately behind would have been a cause for concern if the system had continued. The traction standard at the bottom of Station Road is sited in the garden of the adjacent house. To the rear of 26 is the Station Hotel, which was boarded up at the time of writing, with the triangular corner section having been demolished at an earlier date. (A D Packer)

➜   81. Further along Low Road Sunbeam 24 passes the Three Horse Shoes public house on a sunny day in September 1960, with the faint distant image of the castle in the bright sunlight. The illustrated sign above the right hand door of the pub indicates it is the "Concert Room". The building is now a private residence. (A D Packer)

➜   82. At the same location, vehicles from the joint operators are seen passing each other. On the right, Mexborough's Sunbeam 36 waits before moving towards the Brook Square terminus, whilst Rotherham's Daimler 6 returns to its home town having completed the difficult tight turning manoeuvre. (London Trolleybus Preservation Society)

83.   Two vehicles wait to complete the move to position themselves as indicated in the next picture. The very tight turning circle at Brook Square is well illustrated. The building to the right of the vehicles still exists. (J C Gillham)

84.   Ex Nottinghamshire and Derbyshire English Electric 305, now 69 in the Mexborough and Swinton fleet, pulls in close to the nearside building in Brook Square ready for the tight turn to travel back along Low Road on its return journey to Rotherham. The vehicle looks the worse for wear, possibly from war time neglect, with the cab door open indicating the driver has probably gone to stretch his legs or talk to the conductor. The change to carbon insert skate collectors has still to be made and the vehicle is in the dark red livery with cream band. The area to the right has all been demolished and the road now leads directly to a major junction with the A630, which is controlled by traffic lights. (C C Hall)

85.   The Conisbrough Low terminus at Brook Square is seen here in April 1929 before the property on the left was demolished and with a Garrett, probably 50, waiting to return to towards Mexborough. The H White corner shop has major advertisements for Will's cigarette brands as well as the Waverley brand above the window. Note the corner mounted gas lamp with the photographer's bicycle parked below plus the motorcycle and sidecar in front of the trolleybus. (S L Smith/P Fox copyright)

CONISBROUGH HIGH
(CONANBY)

86.   Sunbeam 33 climbs the very narrow section of Station Road before turning left into Dale Road, which was the beginning of the one-way loop in the castle area and thence onwards to Conanby. Rotherham trolleybuses never operated on this route but their three axle single decker 3 travelled to Conanby on the last day enthusiasts' tour. With no normal Sunday operation it became the last trolleybus to use this section of the system. (R F Mack/J Fozard copyright)

➔ 87.   Sunbeam 37 passes the no entry signs and takes a sharp right hand turn out of Dale Road passed an ex coaching house onto the second section of the one way wiring in Castle Hill in March 1961. A request stop sign is mounted on the nearest traction standard. (S King)

➘ 88. Sunbeam 33 is seen again, this time climbing Castle Hill beside the castle grounds, with the turn out of Dale Road seen in the previous picture at the bottom of the hill. (Photobus)

➔ 89.   Conisbrough Castle, whose fame was spread by Sir Walter Scott's novel "Ivanhoe", forms the backdrop for this view of Sunbeam 37 as it turns out of Castle Hill to then climb Castle Street in April 1960. This location was a favourite spot for enthusiast photographers. In earlier years this narrow road carried two-way traffic before the introduction of the one-way system in 1948. (G Lumb)

90.   A winter scene at the same location depicts Garrett 47 rounding the sharp bend with booms extended and with the castle keep in the misty background. Note the double set of overhead wiring, which provided for two-way traffic before the introduction of the one-way system.
(S Lockwood collection)

91.   Another   fine   view   of Conisbrough Castle with Sunbeam 20 climbing Castle Street on the final section of the one-way loop.
(R F Mack/J Fozard copyright)

92. The upper section of the steep return descent down Station Road from Castle Street was subject to a speed restriction and this was emphasised to drivers via the notice mounted below the bus stop. It read, "M&ST Co Ltd. 5 MPH in upper Station Road". The descent drops down the hill on the left and the building in the background was the local vicarage. The waste bin carries an advertisement for the local coach operations of Whitehead and Sons.
(J C Gillham)

93. In this April 1960 view, Sunbeam 25 enters the short stretch of single wiring at the top of the steep incline to Station Road as it returns to Manvers Main. The overhead wiring coming in from the left provided a short working facility from the Denaby direction. The building to the rear still exists and was previously the Police Station. (A D Packer)

94. Good judgement was required by the drivers of Sunbeams 15 and 16 as they pass each other in Church Street which was widened in 1950. This picture gives another clear view of the rear of the Brush bodywork with emergency exit and boom retainer. (S Lockwood collection)

95.   This April 1960 scene in Old Road near the Conisbrough High terminus again depicts Sunbeam 25 under bracket arm supported overhead, having left the narrow roads around the castle and church behind. On the left is a concrete bus shelter opposite the Lord Conyers Hotel, which is just out of the picture on the left. In the distance is one of the memorable advertisements promoting the strength of Guinness with a bent steel girder to illustrate the claim. (A D Packer)

96.   Two Sunbeams, with 39 at the rear, wait to turn in Welfare Avenue. This was a fairly tight turning circle as indicated by the overhead layout. The last three vehicles to be delivered (JWW registrations) had half drop windows as opposed to the top sliding versions used on earlier post war deliveries. (R F Mack/NTA collection)

97.　　Sunbeam 35 begins the tight turn in Welfare Avenue with the destination blind indicating a depot journey presumably to Old Toll Bar. The leaving passengers begin their walk into the estate; in earlier years they would have been taken further into the estate with the loop around The Crescent. (R F Mack/J Fozard copyright)

98.   Utility Sunbeam 4 has completed the turn in Welfare Avenue under earlier 18" (457 mm) wiring as opposed to the 24" (610mm) spacing in the previous view. Beyond the archway and to the right The Crescent can be seen, although a later arc of shops along Wembley Avenue now exists nearer the photographer. Originally vehicles turned left at the archway and traversed a loop around The Crescent to return into Welfare Avenue from the right. The overhead was cut back to that indicated in 1931. (C Carter)

SPECIAL VEHICLES

99.   Specially prepared for the closure of the system Sunbeam 29, with cut down rear section, approaches Denaby level crossing as it moves towards Mexborough on the 27th March 1961, the day after the system closure. Behind is company Leyland Atlantean 9, and beyond a Burlingham bodied coach, both used to transport guests from Doncaster and to return them, and the band, to the Sheffield Grand Hotel for the commemoration luncheon. The young girl in her mother's arms will probably not remember the event whilst the older gentleman next door may well have travelled regularly on the trolleybuses. (A D Packer)

100.   Another view of this specially prepared trolleybus as it waits in Effingham Street, Rotherham at the junction with Norfolk Street, having discharged the Rawmarsh Prize Band who had travelled in the open rear section. This vehicle headed the closing procession to commemorate 54 years of electrically powered public transport that covered both the tram and trolleybus eras. Standard vehicles followed (32, 33 and 36) in the parade line up. (J Aldridge)

101.   Whoever decided to use Sunbeam 13 as a permanent training vehicle was taking a risk, as potential drivers of a superstitious nature would have had a difficult decision to make. The rear route indicator box has been modified to show the learner driver logo. (R F Mack/J Fozard copyright)

DEPOTS

102.   This view shows the early days of the small Old Toll Bar depot that housed the original trolleybuses plus a limited number of trams. Two of the AEC's, with 26 on the left, can be seen with the tram track curving to the right hand side of the depot. To the rear of the photographer was the turning circle for the original route to Conisbrough. Trolleybuses travelling to the then separate route from Mexborough to Manvers Main, and probably on trips to the Rawmarsh workshops, had to travel from the depot using a trailing skate in the tram track. (S King collection)

103.   The Rawmarsh depot in Dale Road is depicted here with Sunbeam 36 positioned in the forecourt for the photographer and with the destination display indicating Kilnhurst Road Route K. Inside the depot a number of other trolleybuses can be seen and to the right is Leyland TS8 90 purchased from Maidstone and District (SO739) in May 1955, which was eventually converted into a service vehicle. This site was the original depot and workshop for the opening tramway system. (R F Mack/J Fozard copyright)

ROLLING STOCK

104. **1915   21-23   Daimler 21   WT398   (Registered 8/23)**
22/23   WR6822/23   (Registered 1/21)

← These were the first three vehicles to be purchased and were fitted with Brush 26 seat rear entrance bodies. They did not require registration when first introduced and 21 was out of service from 1920 until it was registered in August 1923. Fleet numbers followed on from the tram series and all were withdrawn in 1927. (R Marshall collection)

105.   1917   24   Daimler   WR6824
(Registered 1/21)

← This vehicle was similar to the original batch but purchased second hand from Stockport Corporation. It was new to this municipality in 1913 and was fitted with a 26 seat rear entrance body by Brush who also supplied the motor. The current collection was via the Lloyd-Kohler system which involved pulling a bogie on top of the overhead wiring rather than spring loaded underline collection; Mexborough converted the vehicle to the latter system. Withdrawal came in 1925 and disposal in 1928. Here the vehicle is seen with its original owner numbered 1 in the Stockport fleet; it is suggested that this may be the vehicle purchased by Mexborough.
(Transport and Light Railway/NTA collection)

106.   1922   25-26   AEC   602
WY2743/3059
1924   31   AEC   602
WT7757

25 was previously a demonstrator and all three had chassis numbers that were within the first five of the series. Bodywork was by Strachan & Brown and seated 36 with a rear entrance and motors were thought to have been supplied by BTH. 31 did not enter service until January 1926. All were fitted with pneumatic tyres in 1927 and withdrawal came in 1929/30. One of the three is seen against the industrial background of Manvers Main colliery and with a conductress standing on the bottom entrance step. (S King collection)

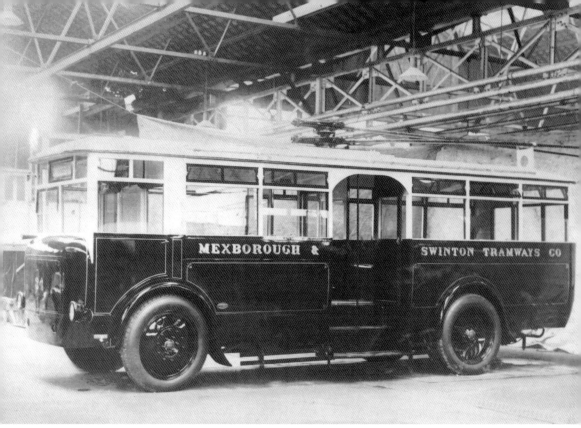

107.	1928	34-39	Garrett O	WW4688-4693
		40-48	Garrett O	WW7872-7880
	1929	49-60	Garrett O	WW8790-8801
	1930	61-63	Garrett O	WX4440-4442

These four batches of vehicles from Garrett were all similar and implemented the tramway replacement programme. They were fitted with Bull 65hp motors and Garrett 32 seat central entrance bodies. First withdrawal was in 1943 (37) and the last in 1950 (42). 40-63 were fitted with front bumpers. This photograph of 34 was taken in the Station Works (also known as Top Works by locals) which was the second manufacturing facility Garrett built in Leiston Suffolk; the building is now part of the Masterlord Industrial Estate. This view was widely used in Garrett's advertising but with the factory background erased. For visitors to East Anglia the Garrett Long Shop Museum is well worth a visit (open April to October). 34 is held at the Sandtoft Transport Centre awaiting restoration. (Garrett Long Shop Museum)

Extract from Garrett sales publicity.

MEXBOROUGH AND SWINTON.

The Mexborough and Swinton Tramways Company operate 2 routes, which are 9½ and 5 miles long respectively, **by a fleet of 27 Garrett Electric Trolley Buses,** and a frequency of service varying from 3 to 15 minutes is maintained, according to the periods of the day. The nature of the routes will show clearly the advantages of the Trolley Bus system as they are of a hilly nature, the maximum gradient being 1 in 7, and they have to traverse narrow and busy streets in Mexborough and Conisbro'. The number of passengers carried for the year 1928 was 6,250,000 ; **current consumption 1.5 units per bus mile.**

Starting Work on Trolleybuses

The Society's Garrett, which is resident at Sandtoft, is one of the oldest trolleybuses in preservation. This report was prepared as a discussion document to work towards securing no. 34's long-term future and refers to the present condition of its bodywork.

RESTORATION OR RECONSTRUCTION?

The Roof

The roof skin is of wooden matchboard construction (with a coated canvas covering) which is in a basically sound condition. The canvas layer is not believed to be a later addition as most of the roof fittings (cable ducting complete with main cables in situ) are undisturbed. Front and rear domes are steel, again covered with canvas which has caused the steel to corrode considerably. The skin is supported on hoops across the whole width of the vehicle at intervals of about two feet. The hoops alternate between wood and wood and steel with the latter tying in to the main body pillars. The steel/wood hoops will probably need replacement as the steel is rusting, causing the hoops to swell. The steel insert continues down into the body pillars with decorated flitch plates inside the saloon.

The Main Body Pillars

The body pillars appear to be of a wood and steel sandwich which displays the same problem (but to a greater extent) as the roof hoops. The steel parts of these have

corroded and swollen to such a degree that it will be difficult to remove any of them so that one can be used as a pattern. All body pillars will require replacement as a matter of course but it should not be too difficult to remanufacture these, once their construction method is ascertained. Initial inspection shows that they are made up as shown below.

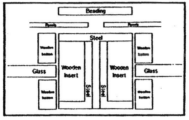

Longitudinal Members

The construction of the longitudinal members varies and it is not possible to ascertain their structure without a certain amount of dismantling - this will not be difficult. Those at roof level, however, seem

to be of 'U'-section steel, again with a wooden insert.

Body Cross-Members

These appear to be basically sound, although the outer ends are likely to be rotten. It may be possible to splice in new sections here; if the body is completely dismantled for restoration, however, it would make sense to replace these as well. Again, these appear to be wooden, with steel inserts and steel reinforcement along their whole length.

Conclusion

Generally, the structure will require complete replacement and only a small number of parts would be suitable for re-use. The fact that the body is not entirely wooden-framed will inevitably cause complications in making the new pillars and other structural members needed for reconstruction. The basic shape of the vehicle, however, is very simple and once the nature of body construction beneath the exterior panels is discovered, work could commence on fabricating parts to build a replica body.

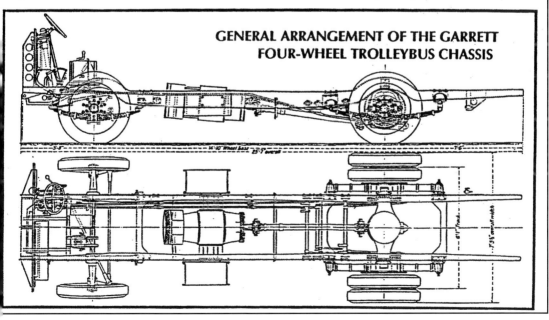

GENERAL ARRANGEMENT OF THE GARRETT FOUR-WHEEL TROLLEYBUS CHASSIS

108.   1937/38   64-69   English Electric   RB5568-5573
These vehicles were new to Nottinghamshire & Derbyshire Traction, a Balfour Beatty subsidiary, in 1932 and were numbered 300-305 in their fleet. English Electric supplied both the motors (60hp) and the bodies that had 32 seats and front entrance. There is a possibility that two of the batch were not into service with Mexborough until early 1938. First withdrawal was in 1943 and two lasted until 1950. 66 is seen at the Rawmarsh depot in post war green and cream livery. (W J Haynes)

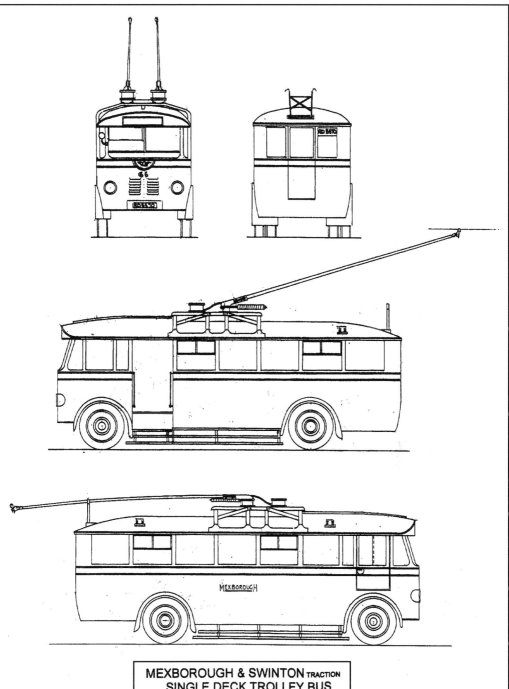

MEXBOROUGH & SWINTON TRACTION
SINGLE DECK TROLLEY BUS

Built : English Electric 1932.	
Fleet No. 64 – 69.	Scale: 4 mm = 1Ft
Bought from Notts & Derby 1937.	

DRAWING No. TB62

DRAWN BY :- TERRY RUSSELL, "CHACESIDE", ST. LEONARDS PARK, HORSHAM, W.SUSSEX. RH13 6EG.
SEND 4 FIRST CLASS STAMPS FOR COMPLETE LIST OF PUBLIC TRANSPORT DRAWINGS.

SCALE
FEET 0 1 2 3 4 5 6 7 8 9 10 11 12

109.   This view depicts one of the English Electric vehicles purchased second hand in 1937 operating with its original owner Nottinghamshire & Derbyshire Traction. Numbered 301 in the latter's fleet it is seen here turning into Thurman Street on the final leg to Hallam Fields resplendent in lined out blue and cream livery. This vehicle became 65 in the Mexborough fleet. Most of the posters on the right are for the erstwhile Daily Herald, the official Labour Party newspaper, whilst the vehicle carries an advertisement for the local Nottingham papers.
(G H F Atkins/Courtesy & © John Banks collection)

110.   1942   70-75   Guy BT 32   DY 5118/5131/5460-61/5579-80

These three axle vehicles were new to the Hastings Tramway Company in 1928/29 being numbered 16/29/47/48/52/53 in their fleet and were purchased by Mexborough to accommodate wartime loadings. Derby Corporation and Nottingham City Transport purchased similar vehicles from Hastings for the same reason. They were fitted with Rees Roturbo 60hp motors and Ransomes Sims and Jeffries 32 seat central entrance bodies. Not all the vehicles purchased by Mexborough entered service but those that did commenced in 1942/43 to be followed by early withdrawal in 1946/47. This rare view depicts 73 (Hastings 48) in Rawmarsh Road about to pass the end of Grafton Bridge with the Rotherham Corporation depot in the background. (Author's collection)

111.　**1943　1-6　Sunbeam W　EWT478-480/513-515**
These utility vehicles were to a Ministry war time specification hence the W chassis designation.
They were fitted with BTH 85hp motors and Brush austerity bodies which included grey livery
when delivered. They were all withdrawn in 1953 and sold to Doncaster Corporation where the
chassis were re-bodied by Roe into double deck format becoming 393-8 in the trolleybus fleet;
they re-entered service in Doncaster in late 1955. The chassis were scrapped in 1962/3 and the
bodies adapted to fit Leyland PD2 motorbus chassis. 1 is seen at the rear of the Rawmarsh depot.
(R F Mack/J Fozard copyright)

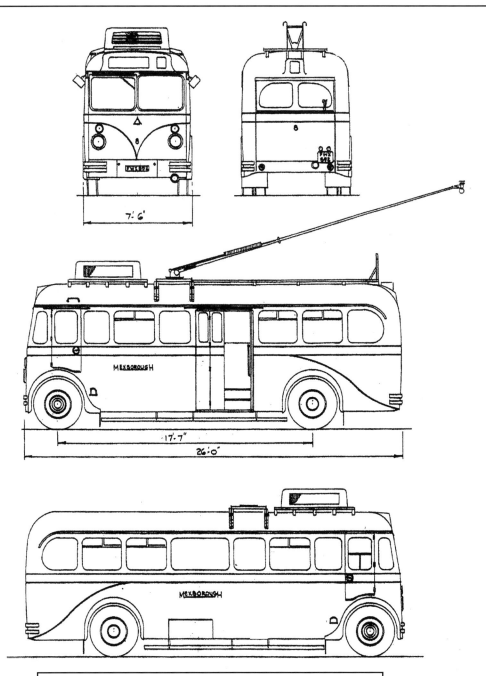

7' 6"

MEXBOROUGH

17'-7"

26'-0"

MEXBOROUGH

The Mexborough fleet all had Brush built bodies, Nos. 7 – 24 on Sunbeam W chassis in 1947, Nos. 25 – 36 in 1947/48 and Nos.37 – 39 in 1950, both batches on Sunbeam F4 chassis. All buses seated 32 and looking at photographs of all batches i would say that all the bodies were virtually identical.   Terry Russell. September 2006

MEXBOROUGH & SWINTON TRACTION
SINGLE DECK TROLLEY BUS

Body: Brush. 1947/50.	
Chassis: Sunbeam W & F4.	Scale: 4 mm = 1Foot.
Fleet No. 7- 36.	

DRAWING No. TB63

DRAWN BY :-TERRY RUSSELL, "CHACESIDE", ST. LEONARDS PARK, HORSHAM, W.SUSSEX. RH13 6EG.
SEND 4 FIRST CLASS STAMPS FOR COMPLETE LIST OF PUBLIC TRANSPORT DRAWINGS.

SCALE
FEET 0   1   2   3   4   5   6   7   8   9   10   11

112.	1947	7-24	Sunbeam W	FWX891-908
	1948	25-36	Sunbeam F4	FWX909-920
	1950	37-39	Sunbeam F4	JWW375-377

These three batches of vehicles were similar other than the chassis specification for the first batch which were fitted with BTH 85hp motors. The rest received motors from the same supplier but rated at 95hp. All were fitted with Brush central entrance 32 seat bodies with the capacity being increased to 35 for the majority during 1955-57. First withdrawal came in 1955 and fourteen lasted until the closure of the system in 1961. Two of the 1947 batch were sold to Doncaster Corporation (becoming their 353/4) who had them re-bodied by Roe as double deckers and introducing them into service in 1958. The chassis were scrapped in 1963 and the bodies adapted to fit Leyland PD2 motorbuses. Two of the 1948 batch were sold to Tees-side Railless Traction in 1961 but were not operated. Nine from the same batch and the entire 1950 batch were sold to Bradford City Transport in 1961 and seven were re-bodied as front entrance double deckers by East Lancashire Coachbuilders and numbered 841-7. They entered service in 1962/3 and were withdrawn in 1971/2; the remainder were used for spares. The West Yorkshire Passenger Transport Executive preserves rebuilt 30 and rebuilt 37-39 are held at the Sandtoft Transport Centre. This unidentified Sunbeam, probably 36, positioned in the forecourt of Rawmarsh depot provides a good side elevation of the post war fleet. Note the manual folding doors.
(R F Mack/J Fozard copyright)

THE BEGINNING AND THE END

113.   This photograph provides an atmospheric view of one of the original Daimler trolleybuses that opened the system, namely 21. It is seen at the original Conisbrough reverser terminus at the junction of Elm Green Lane and Station Road. The photograph was taken in the period before August 1923, as the vehicle does not carry a registration number. The destination is set for the return to Old Toll Bar and the crew, complete with the driver's shiny boots, pose for the photographer. (P Tuffrey collection)

114.   On Monday 27th March 1961, the day after the system closed, a parade of vehicles took place and in this view they are beginning to be assembled at Old Toll Bar with specially prepared Sunbeam 29 heading the ensemble.   It is perhaps appropriate that in the right background the pithead gear of Denaby Main Colliery can be seen, where in the past the colliers from this and other pits in the area used the Mexborough and Swinton trolleybuses at the beginning and end of their shifts. Thus ended nearly 54 years of electric traction through these South Yorkshire towns with the trolleybus system operating for almost 46 of them. (A D Packer)

THE AFTER LIFE

115.   This rear view of utility Sunbeams 5 and 6 was taken at Doncaster Corporation's depot after they had been sold to that municipality in November 1954, together with the other four from the wartime delivery. They were re-bodied as double deckers by Roe and entered service with Doncaster in late 1955 as their 397 and 398. The two illustrated were withdrawn in December 1962 and the bodies transferred to Leyland PD2 motorbuses.
(D A Jones/London Trolleybus Preservation Society)

116.   In this view the chassis of Mexborough and Swinton utility Sunbeam 3 has now received a handsome Roe double deck body and become 395 in the Doncaster fleet entering service in late 1955. The chassis was scrapped in late 1962 and the body adapted to fit a Leyland PD2 motorbus (188), which is now preserved at the South Yorkshire Transport Museum. 395 is seen in West Laithe Gate destined for Balby.
(Author's collection)

117.   Further down the road the chassis of one of the two post war Sunbeams purchased by Doncaster, namely 18, has departed from the Balby stand as 354 having received a double deck body by Roe. It is reported that the single deck bodies were removed at Rawmarsh, one being used as a fibreglass shop by Mexborough. Note the section insulator/power feeder supported from the bracket arm to the rear, as 354 passes a Humber car parked outside the premises of Needle and Stovin. (Author's collection)

118.   Ex Mexborough and Swinton 27 is seen here in immaculate condition as Bradford City Transport 841 at the end of Thornton Road on Route 7 between Thornton and Thornbury. 27 was purchased by Bradford in 1961 and re-bodied by East Lancashire Coachbuilders with front entrance/staircase in 1962. The conductor operates the hand pull to switch the overhead for Market Street as a Renault 10 car overtakes. (D F Parker)

119.   Bradford 846, ex Mexborough and Swinton 38, enters the turning circle at the Thornton terminus with Close Head Lane on the left. This view illustrates the well-proportioned East Lancashire Coachbuilders bodywork specified by Bradford; note how the rear wheels of the original 7' 6" (2.28m) 1950 chassis lay well inside the new 1962 wider body. 846 was one of the few trolleybuses fitted with driver radio communication equipment. (J H Meredith)

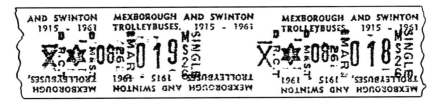

120.   Mexborough and Swinton had the honour of providing at least the chassis of the last operating trolleybus in Bradford and the United Kingdom. Ex Mexborough and Swinton 30, now Bradford 844 after re-bodying in 1962, enters Thornton Road on 26th March 1972 carrying the mayoral party in the closure possession and with a tower wagon in close attendance behind. Bradford operated trolleybuses for 61 years whilst the Mexborough and Swinton system lasted almost 46 years. (D F Parker)

MP Middleton Press

EVOLVING THE ULTIMATE RAIL ENCYCLOPEDIA

Easebourne Lane, Midhurst, West Sussex.
GU29 9AZ   Tel:01730 813169

www.middletonpress.co.uk   email:info@middletonpress.co.uk
A-978 0 906520 B- 978 1 873793 C-978 1 901706 D-978 1 904474 E- 978 1 906008

OOP Out of print at time of printing - Please check availability   BROCHURE AVAILABLE SHOWING NEW TITLES